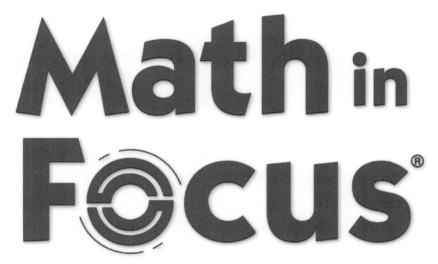

Math in FOCUS®

Singapore Math®
by Marshall Cavendish

Extra Practice
and Homework

Program Consultant
Dr. Fong Ho Kheong

Author
Sophie Shieh

Marshall Cavendish
Education

U.S. Distributor

Houghton Mifflin Harcourt.
The Learning Company™

Grade
KA

© 2020 Marshall Cavendish Education Pte Ltd

Published by Marshall Cavendish Education
Times Centre, 1 New Industrial Road, Singapore 536196
Customer Service Hotline: (65) 6213 9688
US Office Tel: (1-914) 332 8888 | Fax: (1-914) 332 8882
E-mail: cs@mceducation.com
Website: www.mceducation.com

Distributed by
Houghton Mifflin Harcourt
125 High Street
Boston, MA 02110
Tel: 617-351-5000
Website: www.hmhco.com/programs/math-in-focus

First published 2020

ISBN 978-0-358-10296-0

Printed in Singapore

3 4 5 6 7 8 9   1401   26 25 24 23 22
4500840207   B C D E F

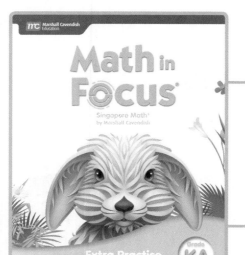

The cover image shows a lop-eared rabbit.
In the wild, rabbits come out at night to feed on grass.
The low light keeps them safe.
Rabbits like to chew on tough things like twigs, bark, and carrots.
This is because their teeth never stop growing!
They chew to keep their teeth short.

Contents

© 2020 Marshall Cavendish Education Pte Ltd

Preface

Welcome!

This is what you will do in **Math in Focus**® *Extra Practice and Homework*.

- Practice what you learn in **Activities**.

- Share your thinking in **MATH JOURNAL**.

- Think hard, as you solve problems in **PUT ON YOUR THINKING CAP!**

Bring home the **SCHOOL-to-HOME CONNECTIONS** letter at the start of each chapter. The letter shows your family what you are learning in school. There are some activities in the letter and your family can do them with you to help you to learn even more!

SCHOOL-to-HOME
CONNECTIONS

Chapter 1

Numbers to 5

Dear Family,

In this chapter, your child will work with numbers to 5. Skills your child will practice include:
- counting, reading, and writing numbers from 0 to 5
- ordering numbers to 5

Math Activities

At the end of this chapter, you may want to carry out these activities with your child. The activities will help to support your child as he or she learns numbers to 5.

Math Talk

Gather 5 identical objects, such as blocks, buttons, or craft sticks. Put 1 object on a table and ask your child to **count** and then say the **number**. Repeat the activity using up to 5 objects. Play more than once, first aligning the objects in a row and then scattering the objects.

Activity 1
- Gather 15 identical objects, such as blocks, buttons, or seashells.
- Use number cards, or write 0, 1, 2, 3, 4, and 5 on separate cards. Shuffle the cards and put them facedown.
- Invite your child to select a card and ask him or her to say the number on the card. Ask your child to select the corresponding number of objects.
- Repeat the above step several times.

Activity 2
- Gather 6 paper plates, 6 clothespins, and 15 identical objects, such as dried beans.
- Write the numbers 0, 1, 2, 3, 4, and 5 on separate clothespins.
- Ask your child to close his or her eyes while you put objects on the plates. Put 1 to 5 objects on each plate. Put the plates in any order.
- Ask your child to open his or her eyes and attach the clothespins to the plates that have a corresponding number of objects.

Activity 3
- Stay indoors or go outdoors to play *I Spy*. Spy 1 of something, then 2 of something, and continue through 5 of something, challenging your child to identify what you see. Then, let your child lead the next round.

SCHOOL
TO HOME

BLANK

Chapter 1

Extra Practice and Homework
Numbers to 5

Activity 1　All About 1 and 2

Match.

 1

Count.
Draw ◯ to show how you count.

 2

 3

Count.
Color to show how many.

Example

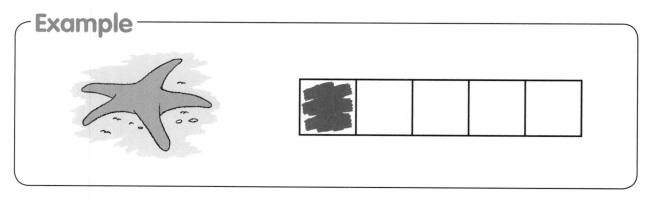

 4

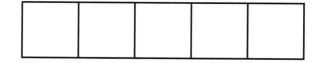

Count and match.

 5

1

2

Trace.
Write each number.

   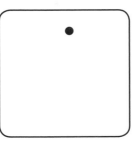 

  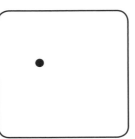

Count and match.

one

two

Circle the groups of 2.

Chapter 1

Extra Practice and Homework
Numbers to 5

Activity 2   All About 3 and 4

Match.

 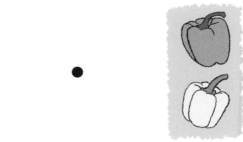

Count.
Color to show how many.

Example

2

3

Count.
Color each box with the correct number.

2	3	4

3	2	1

Trace.
Write each number.

 6

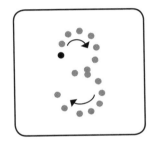 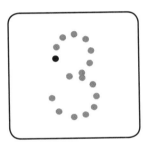 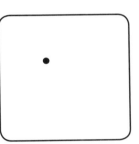 

  7

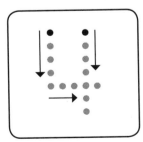 

Count and match.

 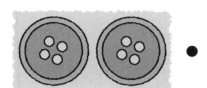

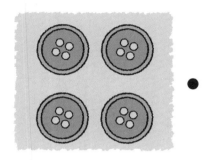 •

•

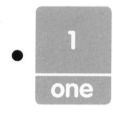 •

•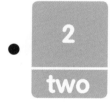

 •

•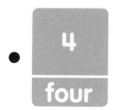

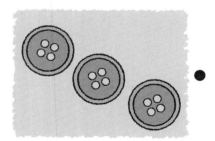 •

Extra Practice and Homework Grade KA

Color four  blue.

Color three ![hanger icon] orange.

Draw.

3 ⬤

4 ▲

Extra Practice and Homework Grade KA

Activity 3   All About 5

Circle the group that shows 5.

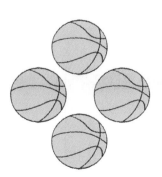

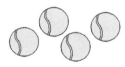

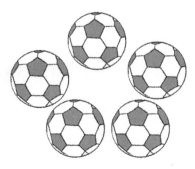

Trace.
Write the number.

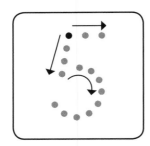  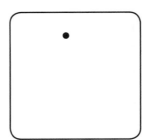 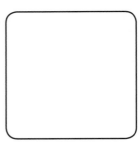

Count.
Write each number.

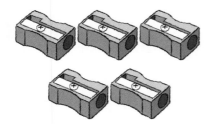

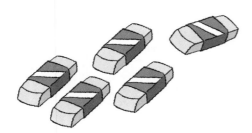

Trace and color 5 ◯.

⭐ 6

One  and five swim in the pond.
Cut out the and glue them below.

7

Extra Practice and Homework Grade KA

Draw to show five .

Find the four kinds of animals in the picture.
Count each kind of animal.
Write each number.

Extra Practice and Homework Grade KA

Activity 4   All About 0

Match.

 •   •

 •   •

 •   •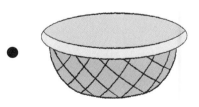

Trace.
Write each number.

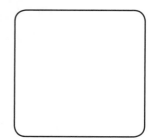

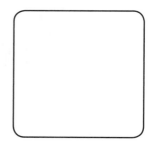

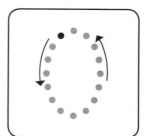

Match.

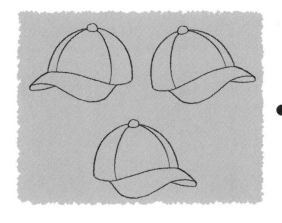 •   •

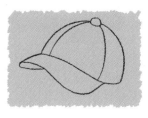 •   •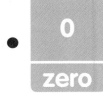

 •   •

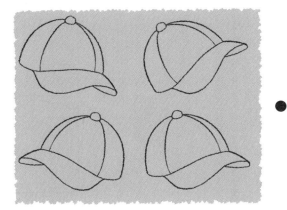 •   •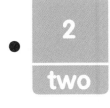

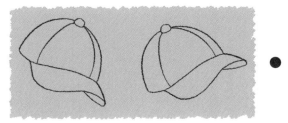

Count.
Write each number.

 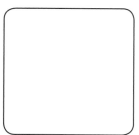 

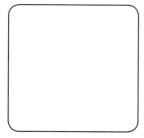 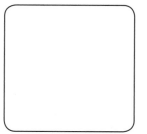

Extra Practice and Homework Grade KA

Chapter 1

Extra Practice and Homework
Numbers to 5

Activity 5　Order Numbers to 5

Write each missing number.

1　1　　3

2　2　　4

3　3　　5

4　4　　2

Write each missing number.

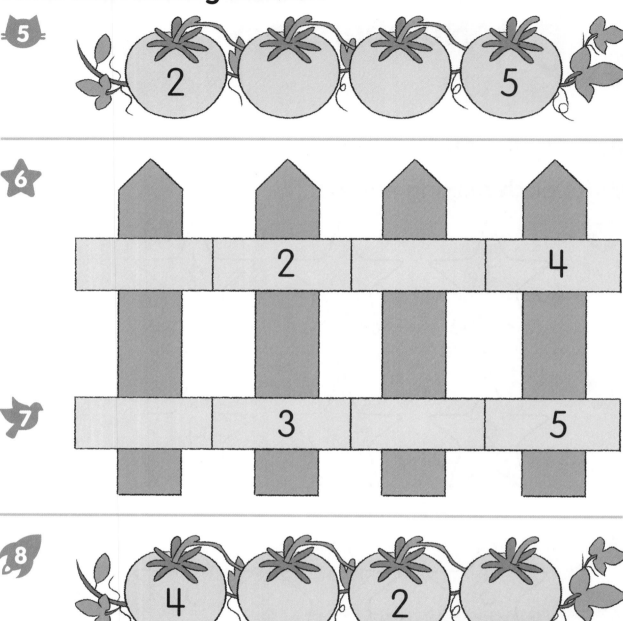

5 🐱 2   5

6 ⭐ 2   4

7 🐦 3   5

8 🚀 4   2

    Extra Practice and Homework Grade KA

Write each missing number.

9   1   2   5

10   4   2

Write each missing number.

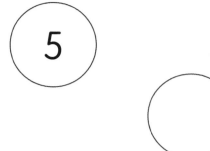

5

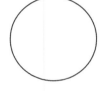

3

1

MATH JOURNAL

1

Mathematical Habit **6** **Use precise mathematical language**

Use ◯ to make a story about numbers to 5.

Tell your story to your partner.

2 **Mathematical Habit 6** Use precise mathematical language

Look at these numbers.

1

0   4   3

2   5

Circle the number you like best.
Tell your partner about it.

Extra Practice and Homework Grade KA

Mathematical Habit 4 Use mathematical models

Carla draws 5 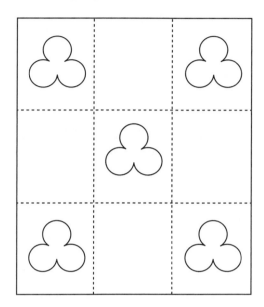 on the card below.

What are two other ways to show 5?
Draw and color them.

Way 1

Way 2

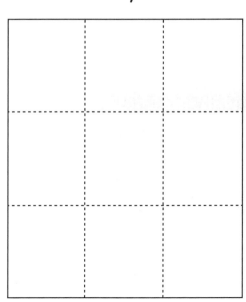

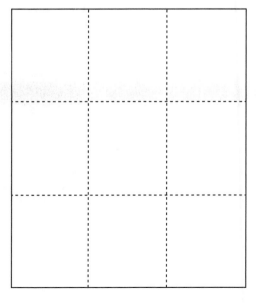

UT ON YOUR THINKING CAP!

2 **Mathematical Habit 1** **Persevere in solving problems**

Which nest has 5 eggs?
Color it.

SCHOOL-to-HOME
CONNECTIONS

Numbers to 10

Dear Family,

In this chapter, your child will work with numbers to 10. Skills your child will practice include:

- counting, reading, and writing numbers from 6 to 10
- ordering numbers to 10
- making number pairs to 10
- using ordinal numbers to tell order

Math Activities

At the end of this chapter, you may want to carry out these activities with your child. The activities will help to support your child as he or she learns numbers to 10.

Activity 1

- Gather 40 identical objects such as dried beans or paper clips and 5 transparent plastic cups or paper plates.
- Write the numbers 6, 7, 8, 9, and 10 on separate cups or plates.
- Place the corresponding number of objects in each cup or on each plate.
- Count aloud as you work.
- Empty the cups or plates before your child leads the next round.

 **Math Talk**

Gather 10 identical objects, such as blocks or buttons. Put 6 objects on a table and ask your child to **count** and then say the **numbers**. Repeat the activity using up to 10 objects. Play more than once, first aligning the objects in a row and then scattering the objects.

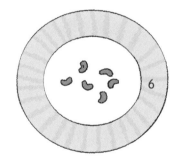

Activity 2

• Use sidewalk chalk to draw a hopscotch pattern on a flat surface, or visit a playground where a hopscotch pattern already exists. Toss a pebble, button, or some other object and call out the numbers in order as you hop. Then, let your child play the next round.

10

9

7   8

6

4   5

3

2

1

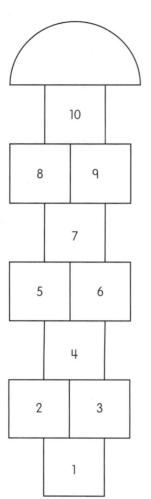

10

8   9

7

5   6

4

2   3

1

Chapter 2

Extra Practice and Homework
Numbers to 10

Activity 1   All About 6 and 7

Match.

  · ·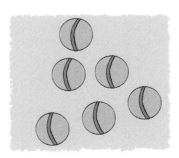

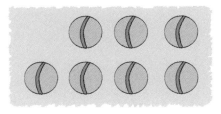 · ·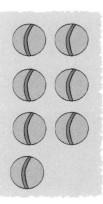

Color to show 6.

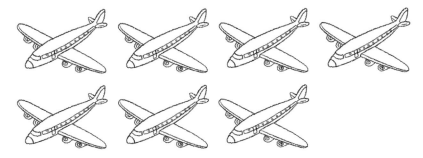

Count.
Color to show how many.

 3

Count.
Color the correct box.

 4

6
7

Trace.
Write each number.

 5

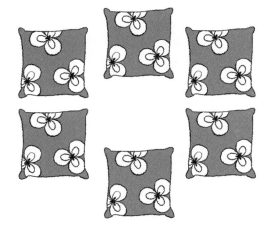

6   6   •

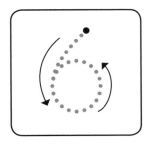 **6**

7   7   •

Color seven  red.

Color six green.

Match.

•

• seven

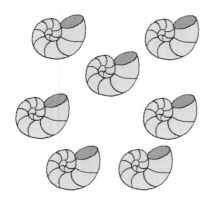

•

• six

Activity 2 All About 8 and 9

Count.
Color to show how many.

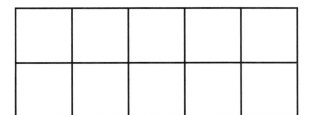

Count.
Color to show how many.

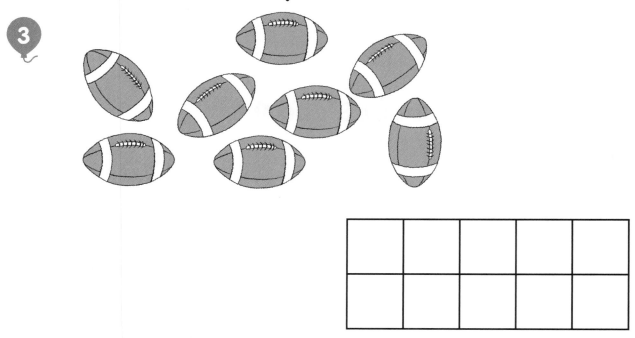

Count.
Color the box with the correct number.

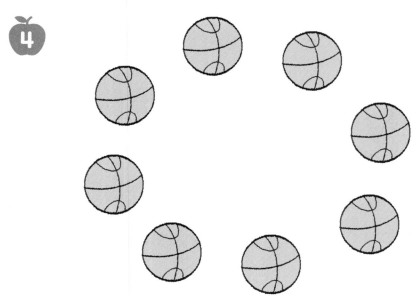

7	8	9

Trace each number.

 5

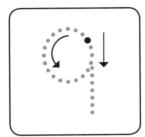 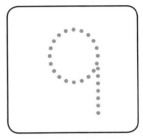

 6

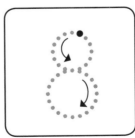 

Color eight ♡ red.
Color nine 🐋 blue.

Show 8  on the bag.
Cut out the ⭐ and glue them below.

Count and match.

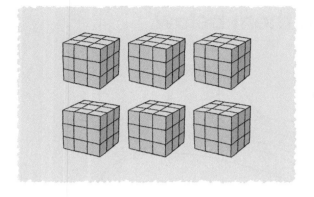

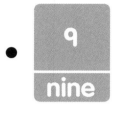

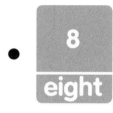

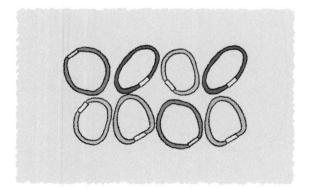

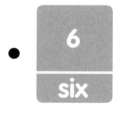

Activity 3   All About 10

Count.
Color to show how many.

1

2

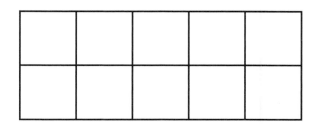

Count.
Color the box with the correct number.

| 8 | 9 | 10 |

Trace.
Write the number.

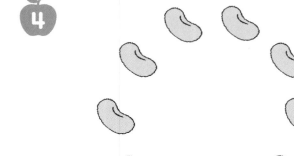

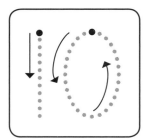
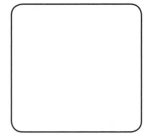

Count.
Write the number.

5

6

Count.
Match.

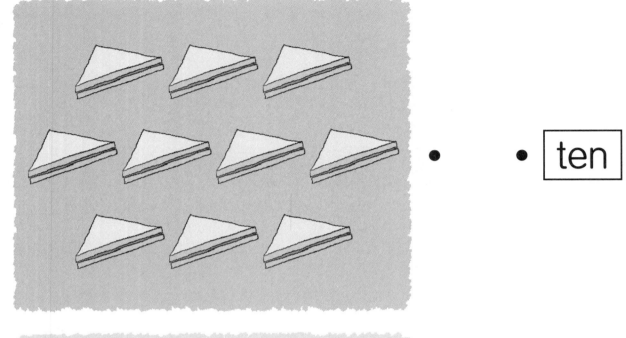

•   • ten

•   • nine

Extra Practice and Homework Grade KA

Chapter 2

Extra Practice and Homework
Numbers to 10

Activity 4   Order Numbers to 10

The numbers are in order.
Write each missing number.

 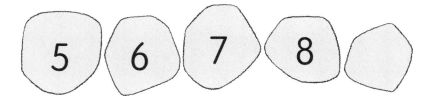

5   6   7   8   ___

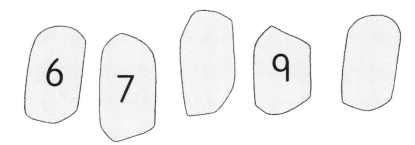

6   7   ___   9   ___

 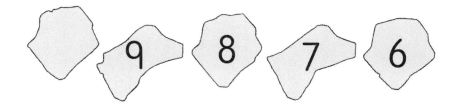

___   9   8   7   6

 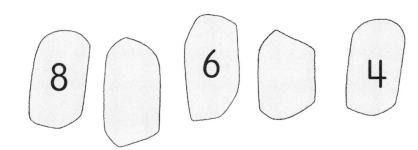

8   ___   6   ___   4

Connect the dots in order.

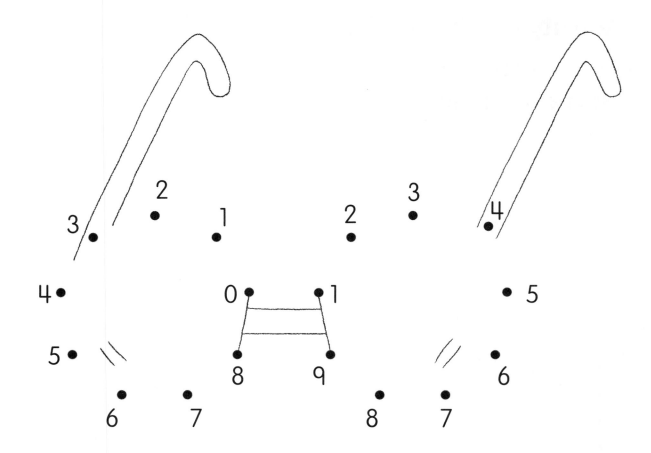

Chapter 2

Extra Practice and Homework
Numbers to 10

Activity 5   Make Number Pairs to 10

Color to make number pairs.
Fill in each blank.

 a

1 and 2 make _____.

b

3 and 0 make _____.

c

1 and 1 make _____.

What numbers make 4?
Fill in each blank.

  a

3 and 1 make _____.

b

2 and 2 make _____.

c

4 and 0 make _____.

Extra Practice and Homework Grade KA

What numbers make 5?
Use 2 colors to show.
Write each number.

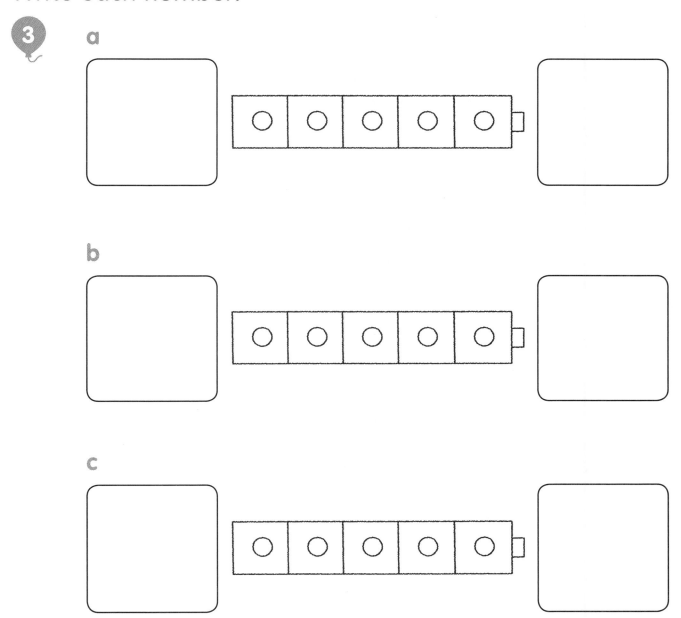

3   a

   b

   c

What numbers make 6?
Use 2 colors to show.
Fill in each blank.

 a

_____ and _____ make 6.

b

_____ and _____ make 6.

What numbers make 7?
Use 2 colors to show.
Fill in each blank.

 a

_____ and _____ make 7.

b

_____ and _____ make 7.

c

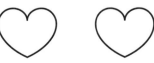

_____ and _____ make 7.

What numbers make 8?
Use 2 colors to show.
Fill in each blank.

 a

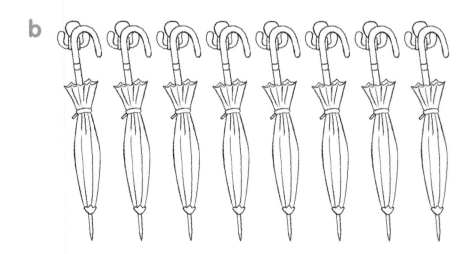

_____ and _____ make 8.

b

_____ and _____ make 8.

What numbers make 9?
Fill in each blank.

 a

_____ and _____ make 9.

b

_____ and _____ make 9.

c

_____ and _____ make 9.

d

_____ and _____ make 9.

What numbers make 10?
Use 2 colors to show.
Fill in each blank.

  a

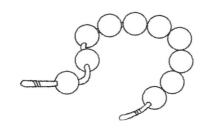

_____ and _____ make 10.

b

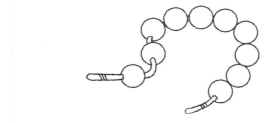

_____ and _____ make 10.

c

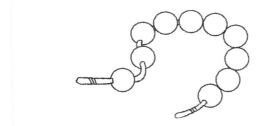

_____ and _____ make 10.

d

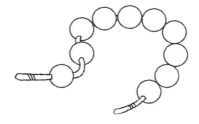

_____ and _____ make 10.

Chapter 2

Extra Practice and Homework
Numbers to 10

Activity 6   Ordinal Numbers

Circle.

 the 4th pencil

1st

 the 3rd shoe

1st

Make an ✗ on the 5th .

1st

The firemen are climbing up.
Fill in each blank.
Write 3rd, 4th, or 5th.

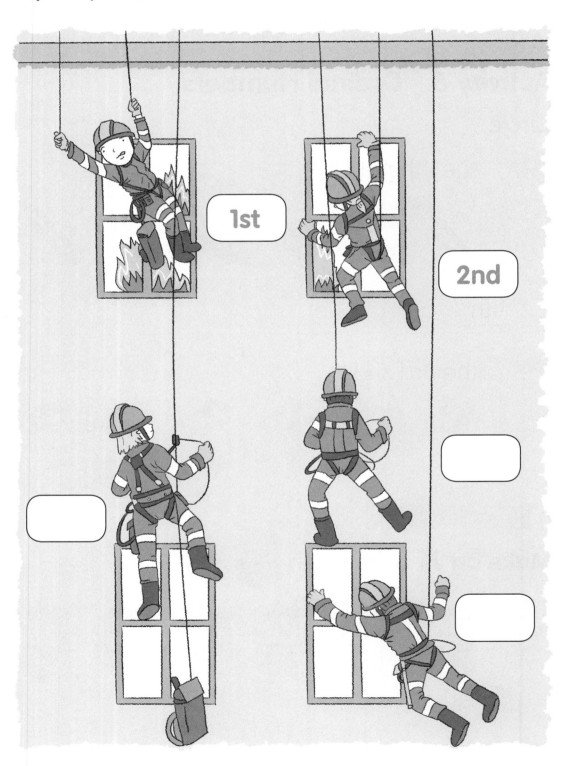

Mathematical Habit 2 Use mathematical reasoning

Look at the picture below.
Some people are waiting for a taxi.
Color the correct box.

a   How many people are waiting?

10	7	5

b   Fill in each blank.
Use the words in the box.

| 4th   2nd   1st   5th |

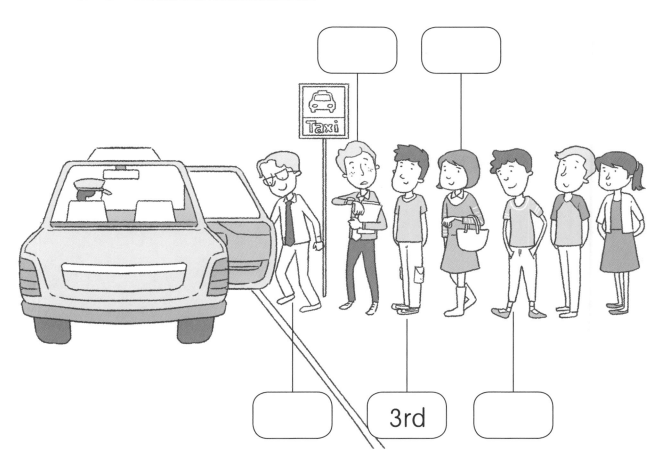

3rd

1 Mathematical Habit **2** Use mathematical reasoning

Draw to make 8.
Circle to show number pairs.
Fill in each blank.

Way 1

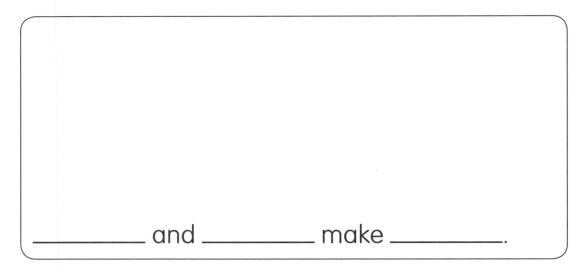

_____ and _____ make _____.

Way 2

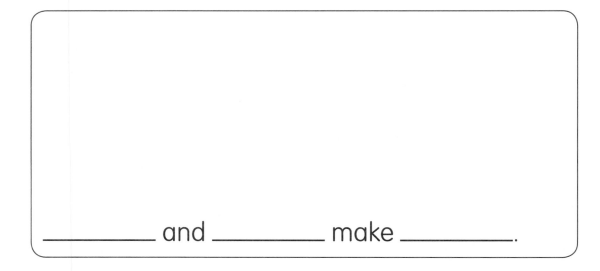

_____ and _____ make _____.

SCHOOL-to-HOME
CONNECTIONS

Chapter 3

Measurement

Dear Family,

In this chapter, your child will learn about measurement. Skills your child will practice include:
- comparing the lengths of two objects
- measuring length using non-standard units
- comparing the heights of two objects
- measuring height using non-standard units
- comparing the weights of two objects

Math Activities

At the end of this chapter, you may want to carry out these activities with your child. The activities will help to support your child as he or she learns about measurements.

Activity 1

- Take a few uncooked spaghetti noodles and break them into different lengths.
- Ask your child to choose two pieces of uncooked spaghetti noodles and compare their lengths.
- Have your child identify which piece of uncooked spaghetti noodle is shorter and which piece of uncooked spaghetti noodle is longer.
- Repeat the activity several times.
- Have your child order the pieces of uncooked spaghetti noodles from shortest to longest and then from longest to shortest.

Activity 2

- Visit a library to read books together about measuring length and weight, such as *Length* by Henry Arthur Pluckrose, *Actual Size* by Steve Jenkins, and *Mighty Maddie* by Stuart Murphy.

Math Talk

Ask your child to gather a collection of toys. Have your child hold two objects and compare their weights, identifying which object is **heavier** and which object is **lighter**. Continue comparing the weights of different pairs of toys. Then ask your child to compare the lengths and heights of objects to determine which are **longer** and which are **shorter**, and which are **taller** and which are **shorter**.

Activity 3

- Make a homemade balance using a ruler and an empty toilet roll as shown below. Paste scotch tape as shown in the picture. Balance the ruler on top of the empty toilet roll. Then, use it to compare weights.
- Have your child add 1 object to one side of the ruler while you add a different object to the other side at the same time. Talk about which object is heavier or lighter, or whether they weigh the same.

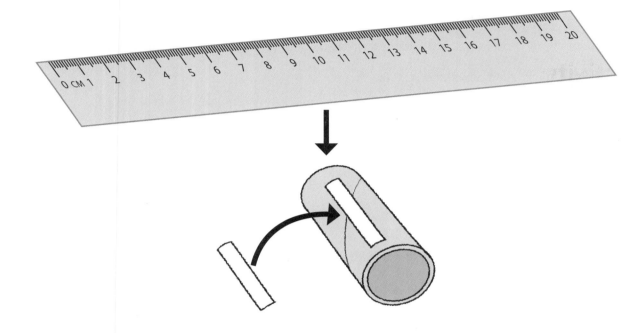

Chapter 3

Extra Practice and Homework
Measurement

Activity 1   Compare Lengths
Draw a long line.

Draw a short line.

Color the longer .
Circle the shorter .

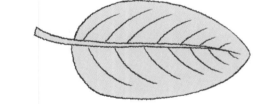

Which have the same length?
Circle them.

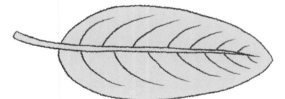

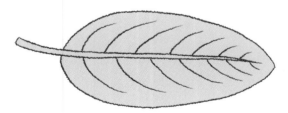

Draw a line that is shorter than the .

Draw a line that is as long as the .

Color the ☐ to show the lengths.

7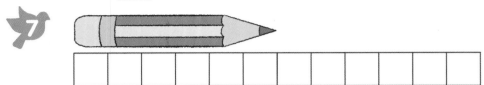

8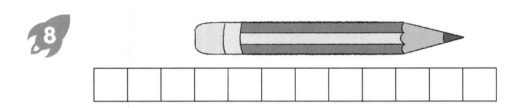

Count the ▭ or ◠.
Fill in each blank.

9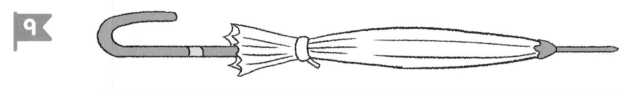

The umbrella is about _____ ▭ long.

10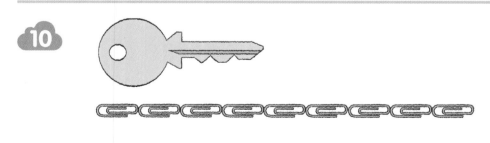

The key is about _____ ◠ long.

Chapter 3

Extra Practice and Homework
Measurement

Activity 2   Compare Heights

Draw a tall tree.

Draw a short tree.

Who is taller?
Color.

Make an ✗ on the shorter tree.
If they have the same height, circle them both.

Which is shorter?
Make an ✖ on it.

Color the correct box.

A   B

Cup A is
| taller than |
| as tall as |
| shorter than |
Cup B.

Count the  **or** ⬜ **.**

Fill in each blank.

It is about _____  tall.

It is about _____ ⬜ tall.

Activity 3   Compare Lengths, Heights, and Weights

Which animals are light?
Circle them.

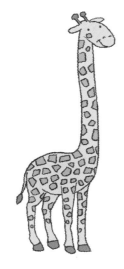

Which is heavier? Color it.
Which is lighter? Make an ✘ on it.

Which is shorter? Color it.
Which is heavier? Circle it.

Which is taller? Circle it.
Which is heavier? Color it.

5

Which is longer? Make an ✖ on it.
Which is lighter? Circle it.

6

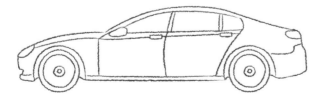

Draw a longer and taller bag.

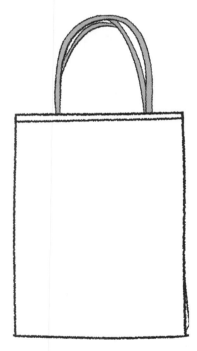

Name: _____ Date: _____

Mathematical Habit 6 **Use precise mathematical language**

Make a story from the picture.
Use words from the box.
Tell your story to your partner.

| taller | lighter | heavier | longer | shorter |

2 | **Mathematical Habit 5 Use tools strategically**

Look at the cats.
Which cat is taller?
Tell your partner how to show this.
Color the correct box.

A   B

Cat A is
| taller than |
| as tall as |
| shorter than |
Cat B.

1 Mathematical Habit **2** Use mathematical reasoning

How tall is Giraffe B?

A   B

My guess: _____

2 **Mathematical Habit 1 Persevere in solving problems**

Daniel has objects A, B, and C.

Each object will have a .

Read the clues.

Match each object to the correct .

Clues:

A is longer than B.

A is lighter than B.

C is lighter than B.

C is longer than A.

• • •

• • •

 A   B   C

SCHOOL-to-HOME
CONNECTIONS

Chapter 4

Compare Numbers to 10

Dear Family,

In this chapter, your child will compare numbers to 10. Skills your child will practice include:
- comparing two sets of objects using the same
- comparing two sets of objects using greater than
- comparing two sets of objects using less than
- comparing two numbers to 10
- identifying 1 more or 1 less from a number

Math Activities

At the end of this chapter, you may want to carry out these activities with your child. The activities will help to support your child as he or she compares numbers to 10.

Math Talk

Gather some stacking blocks or snap cubes. Make two towers, 1 to 5 blocks tall. Ask your child to help you compare the number of blocks in each tower, using the words **the same**, **greater than**, or **less than**. Repeat the activity several times, letting your child build and compare the towers each time.

Activity 1

- Gather 20 identical objects such as dried beans or paper clips and 2 paper plates. Keep one paper plate for yourself, and give the other paper plate to your child.
- Use number cards, or write the numbers 0 to 10 on separate cards. Shuffle the cards and put them facedown.
- Select a card, read the number aloud, put the corresponding number of objects on your plate, and place the number card in front of the plate. Then, have your child do the same. Use the words *the same*, *greater than*, or *less than* to compare the numbers. Return the objects and the cards before your child leads the next round.

Activity 2

- Gather a handful of beads or cereal hoops and 2 pipe cleaners.
- Ask your child to thread 0 to 5 beads or cereal hoops onto a pipe cleaner while you do the same, without looking at each other's work.
- Reveal your work to each other when both of you have completed your work. Use the words *the same*, *greater than*, or *less than* to compare the number of objects on the pipe cleaners.
- Return the objects before playing again.

SCHOOL
TO HOME

BLANK

Chapter 4 — Extra Practice and Homework
Compare Numbers to 10

Activity 1   More Than

Match each to a .

Circle the group that has more.

 1

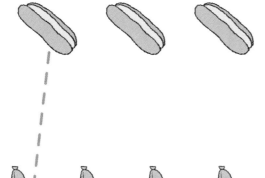

 2

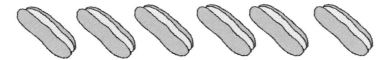

Match each to a .

Circle the group that has more.

 (flowers)

Match and compare.
Circle the group that has more.

Extra Practice and Homework Grade KA

Match and compare.
Color each correct box.

 5

There are more than .

There are more than .

 6

There are more than .

There are more than .

Answer each question.

a Draw more ⬭ than 🐚 .

b How many ⬭ did you draw?

Answer each question.

a Draw more than .

b How many ◯ did you draw?

Compare.
Circle the group that has more.

Extra Practice and Homework Grade KA

Activity 2   Fewer Than

Match each to a .

Circle the group that has fewer.

Match and compare.
Color each correct box.

 2

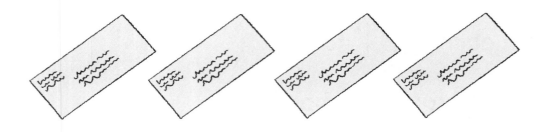

There are
more
fewer
   than .

 3

There are
more
fewer
 than .

Extra Practice and Homework Grade KA

Compare.
Circle the group that has fewer.

 4

 5

Answer each question.

 6

a Draw fewer than  .

b How many did you draw?

Activity 3   Same

Match and compare.
Color the correct box.

 1

There are more than .

The number of and is the same.

Match and compare.
Color the correct box.

Is the number of 🐭 and 🍓 the same?

Yes
No

Compare.
Circle all the groups with the same number.

Compare.
Color the correct boxes.

 4

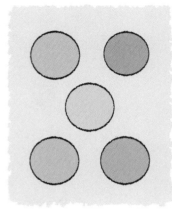  

The number of   and

is the same.

 5

 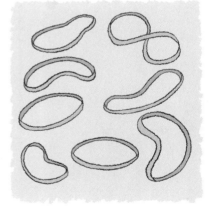 

The number of 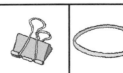 and

is the same.

Compare.
Match the groups that show the same number.

   •   •

   •   •

   •   •

   •   •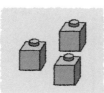

Extra Practice and Homework Grade KA

Compare Numbers to 10

Activity 4   Compare Numbers to 10

Write each number.

 1

Color each correct box.

 2 There are
more
fewer
 than  .

 3 3 is
less than
greater than
5.

Write each number.

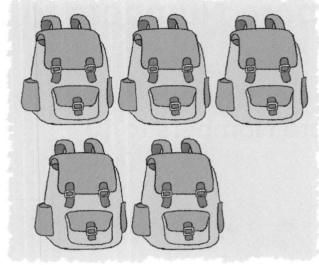

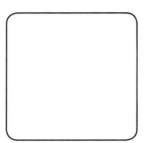

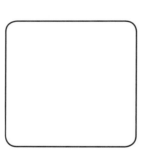

Compare the numbers.
Color each correct box.

 There are
more
fewer
 than .

 6 is
greater than
less than
5.

Extra Practice and Homework Grade KA

Circle the numbers that are less than 5.

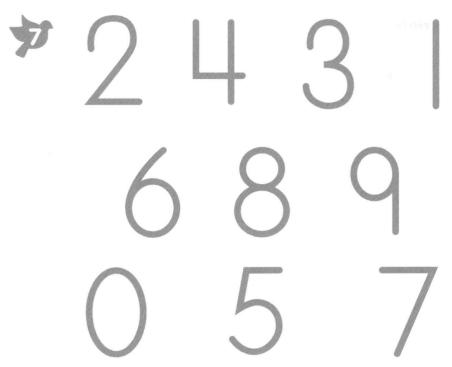

7 2 4 3 1

6 8 9

0 5 7

Compare and color.

 8 is
greater than
the same as
less than
4.

---

 9 is
greater than
the same as
less than
9.

Write each number.
Circle the group that has 1 more.

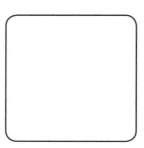

Fill in each blank.

 _____ is 1 more than 4.

 _____ is 1 less than 5.

Write each number.
Circle the group that has 1 less.

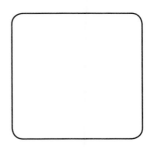

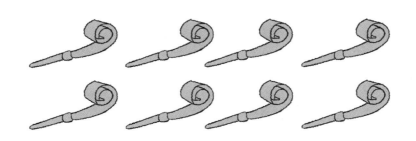

Fill in each blank.

 1 less than 9 is _____.

 _____ is 1 less than 9.

Count.
Write.
Draw.

a There are  .

b Draw  to show 1 more.

c How many  did you draw?

Extra Practice and Homework Grade KA

Name: _____ Date: _____

Mathematical Habit 6 Use precise mathematical language

Look at the picture.
Color the correct boxes.

a There is ┌─────────┐ than 🐑.
           │ 1 more │
           │ 1 less │ 🦆
           └─────────┘

b The number of 🐦 is ┌─────────┐ than 5.
                       │ 1 less │
                       │ 1 more │
                       └─────────┘

c The number of 🐴 is ┌────────────────┐ the
                       │ the same as   │
                       │ less than   │
                       └────────────────┘

number of 🐄.

Mathematical Habit 2 Use mathematical reasoning

Draw ( ) to show the same number of .

Extra Practice and Homework Grade KA

Mathematical Habit 1 Persevere in solving problems

Luis has some .

The number of  is greater than 2.

It is also less than 5.

Draw the  that Luis has.

There is more than 1 answer!

2 | **Mathematical Habit 2** Use mathematical reasoning

Match.

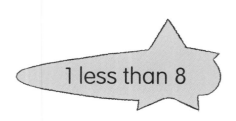

Chapter 5

Flat and Solid Shapes

Dear Family,

In this chapter, your child will learn about flat shapes and solid shapes. Skills your child will practice include:
- identifying, naming, and describing flat and solid shapes
- recognizing flat and solid shapes in real life
- using position words to name relative positions of shapes
- combining shapes together to form new shapes
- analysing and comparing shapes
- using flat and solid shapes to identify and extend shape patterns

Math Activities

At the end of this chapter, you may want to carry out these activities with your child. The activities will help to support your child as he or she learns about shapes.

Activity 1
- Visit a library to read books together about shapes, such as *Skippyjon Jones shape up* by Judy Schachner, *Shape by Shape* by Suse MacDonald, and *Not a Box* by Antoinette Portis.

Activity 2
- Play *I Spy a Shape*, looking for examples of flat shapes and solid shapes in your home. For example, you may find flat circular, square, rectangular, hexagonal, and triangular snack crackers and solid boxes, cylindrical cans, and ice cream or party hat cones.
- Make a list of your findings and encourage your child to help to continue adding new objects to the list as you find them.

Activity 3
- Use store-bought or homemade dough to make assorted solid shapes, such as cones, spheres, cubes, and cylinders.
- Encourage your child to combine different shapes to make an animal, vehicle, building, or other interesting possibilities and then tell a story about it.

Math Talk

Gather some straws and marshmallows. Use the straws to help your child make assorted flat shapes, such as squares, rectangles, and triangles. Talk about the shapes' features, such as the **number of sides** and the **number of corners**. Then use the straws or parts of straws to make and talk about solid shapes, such as cubes, cylinders, and cones. Use marshmallows to join the straws.

BLANK

Name: _____ Date: _____

Activity 1 Flat Shapes
Color each correct shape.

 1 | circle |

---

 2 | triangle |

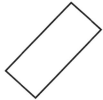

---

 3 | rectangle |

Color the box with the name of each shape.

 4

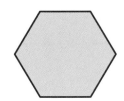

| circle | hexagon |

 5

| square | triangle |

Match.

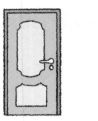 •

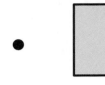 •

 •

  •

 •

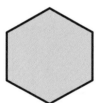
  •

 •

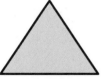
  •

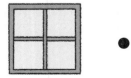 •

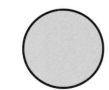
  •

Chapter 5

Extra Practice and Homework
Flat and Solid Shapes

Activity 2 Solid Shapes

Circle each correct shape.

 1 | cube |

 **2** | cone |

Color the box with the name of each shape.

 3

| sphere | cone |

 4

| sphere | cylinder |

Which solid shape is it?
Use these colors for the shapes.

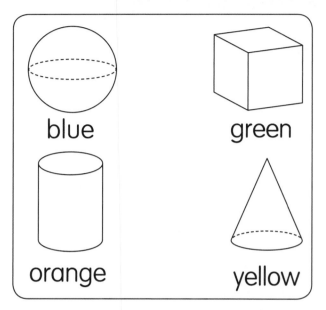

blue   green

orange   yellow

 5

      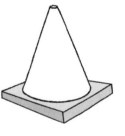

   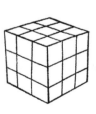   

Which can roll? Make an ✗ on them.
Which can slide? Circle them.

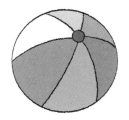 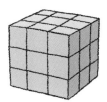

 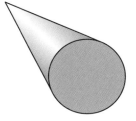

Which can roll and stack on other shapes?
Circle them.

 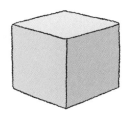 

Which shapes can stack on themselves? Circle them.

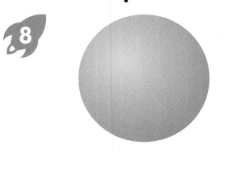

Which shapes can slide and stack on themselves? Circle them.

Extra Practice and Homework Grade KA

Chapter 5

Extra Practice and Homework
Flat and Solid Shapes

Activity 3   Positions

Color.

1 a the **beside** the 🌳

b the 🌿 **behind** the 🪑

c the 🐰 **in front of** the 🧒

Circle.

 What is **in front of** the ?

What is its shape?   cylinder   cone

3 What is **below** the ?

What is its shape?   sphere   cube

 4 What is **next to** the ?

What is its shape?   rectangle   sphere

 5 What is **beside** the ?

What is its shape?   cylinder   cone

 6 What is **behind** the ?

What is its shape?   cone   cube

Draw the object.
Color the correct box.

 7 Draw a **beside** the .

What is its shape?

cylinder	cone

 8 Draw a △ **above** the .

What is its shape?

circle	triangle

Activity 4   Make New Shapes

Circle the shapes used to make each shape.

 1

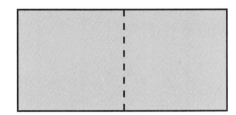

 2

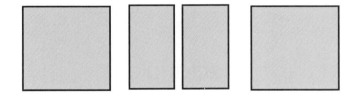

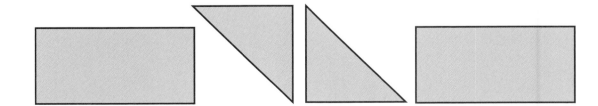

Color the correct number of shapes.

 3 What shapes make this triangle?

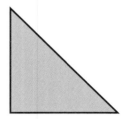   

 4 What shapes make this hexagon?

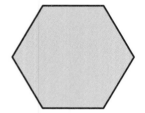   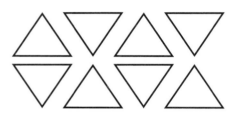

 5 What shapes make this rectangle?

   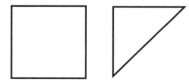

Draw lines to show how you make the shapes shown.

 2

 2

 4

Count.
Fill in each blank.

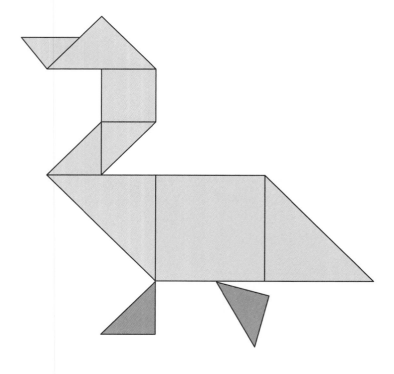

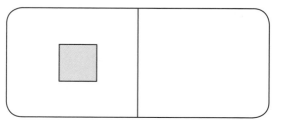

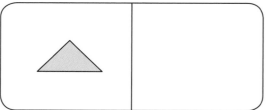

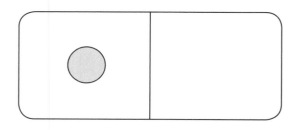

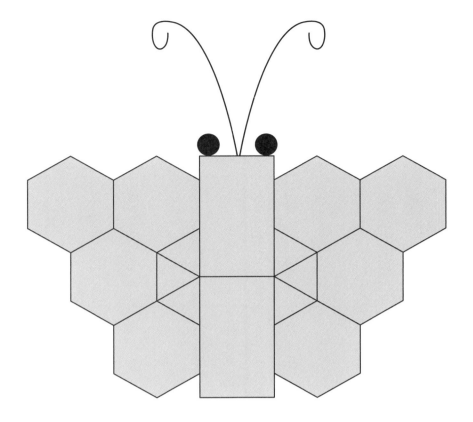

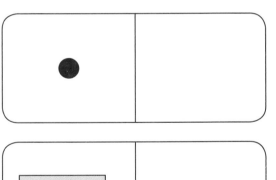

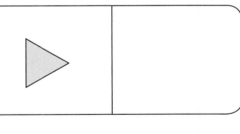

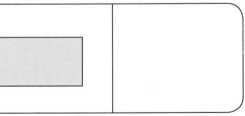

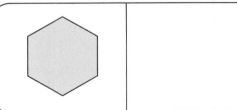

Circle the shapes used.

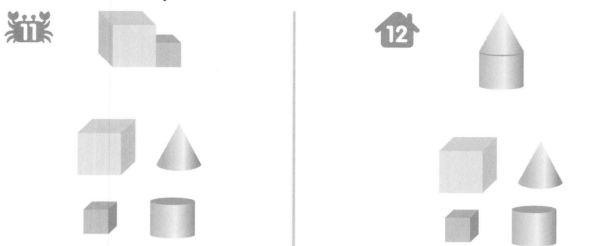

Count.
Fill in each blank.

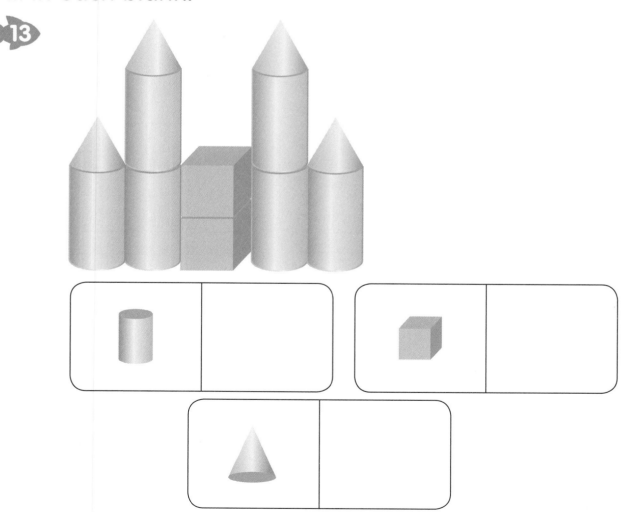

Extra Practice and Homework
Flat and Solid Shapes

Activity 5 Compare Flat and Solid Shapes

Color the correct box.

A square has | 2 | 3 | 4 | sides.

A square has | 2 | 3 | 4 | corners.

A hexagon has | 6 | 7 | 8 | sides.

A hexagon has | 6 | 7 | 8 | corners.

A triangle has | 2 | 3 | 4 | sides.

A triangle has | 2 | 3 | 4 | corners.

Circle shapes with 3 corners.
Color shapes with 4 sides green.

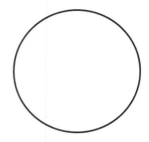
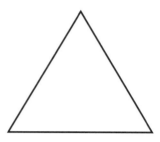
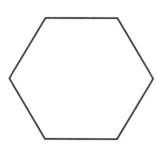

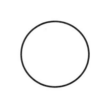

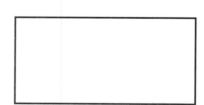
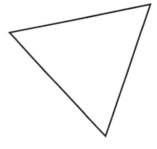
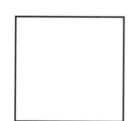

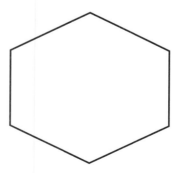
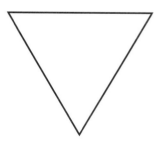

Draw.

 5 A shape with 4 corners.

 6 A shape with 3 sides.

Which words describe each shape?
Color the boxes with these words.

 7

flat face
curved surface

 **8**

flat face
curved surface

Which shapes have flat faces?
Circle them.
Which shapes have curved surfaces?
Make an X on them.

Extra Practice and Homework Grade KA

Activity 6   Shape Patterns
What shape comes next?
Color it.

 1

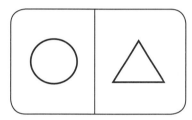

 2

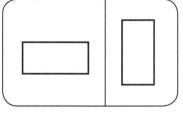

 3

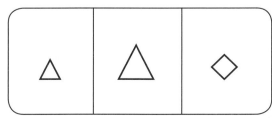

What is the missing shape?
Circle it.

4 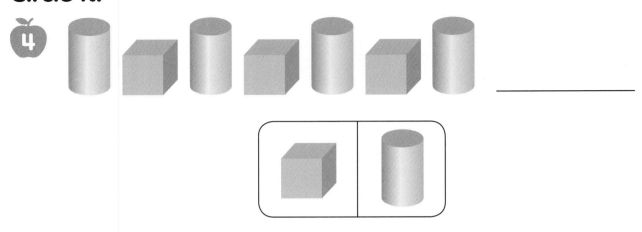 _____

5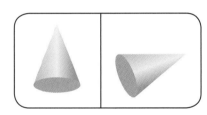

6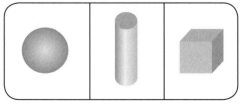

Name: _____ Date: _____

Mathematical Habit 6 **Use precise mathematical language**

a What solid shape do you like the most?
Circle it.

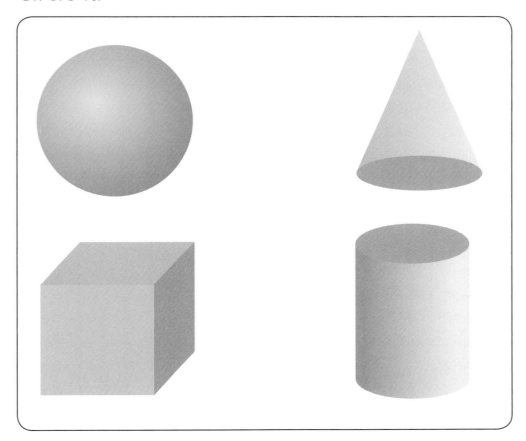

b Find an object with this shape.
Tell your partner about it.
Use words from the box.

curved surface	flat face
slide	roll
stack on itself	stack on other solid shapes

1 `Mathematical Habit` **6** **Use precise mathematical language**

I can roll and slide.
I have one flat surface.

What shape am I?
Color the correct box.

| cylinder |
| sphere |
| cone |

---

 2 `Mathematical Habit` **1** **Persevere in solving problems**

Count. Fill in each blank.

triangle   _____

rectangle   _____

circle   _____

square   _____